grins and giggles

"Ahhh, What's Up Doc?"

Simply Silly!

Surprise your kids with a special everyday snack or create fun party memories with a plateful – then watch the grins appear!

Supplies to make it easy:
- Pastry bags fitted with tips (Or, spoon frosting into plastic sandwich bags, cut off a small corner and squeeze the bag. The smaller the hole, the finer the piped lines.)
- Ready-to-use frostings and icings in tubs, tubes or cans
- Toothpicks (to apply bits of frosting and melted bark)
- Tweezers (to handle small pieces)
- Offset spatula
- Small metal cookie cutters

Copyright © 2013 CQ Products
Waverly, IA 50677
All rights reserved.
No part of this book may be reproduced or transmitted in any form or by any means, electronic or mechanical, including photocopying, recording or by any information storage and retrieval system, without permission in writing from the publisher.

Printed in the United States of America
by G&R Publishing Co.

Distributed By:

507 Industrial Street
Waverly, IA 50677

ISBN-13: 978-1-56383-450-9
ISBN-10: 1-56383-450-2
Item #7088

Rainbow Goldfish

Dried mango, pineapple and kiwifruit

Baby carrots, grape tomatoes and broccoli florets

Flutterbies

Use scissors to cut jumbo colored craft sticks slightly longer than a wooden clothespin. Hot-glue one stick to each clothespin, rounded end in front. Glue on wobbly plastic eyeballs near rounded end. Fill zippered plastic snack bags with small crackers or vegetables, dried fruit, grapes, cereal, mini colored marshmallows or assorted small candies, leaving some space. Seal bags, gather center to form two wings and clip with clothespin. For antennae, twist colored chenille stems together and cut to 6˝ long; insert in clothespin and bend ends up.

Cookie Critter Cuties

You'll Need

Round sugar or chocolate cookies*

White frosting

Candy eyeballs

and..

For Pandas: white sparkling sugar or nonpareils, dark chocolate Kisses, chocolate decorating sprinkles

For Puppies: brown peanut M&Ms, red Rips candy, pink jelly beans, small Tootsie Rolls (unwrapped)

For Chicks: yellow decorating sugar, yellow candy wafers, orange Warhead Sour Chewy Cubes

Make It

Panda

Spread frosting generously on cookie. Dip frosting side of cookie into sparkling sugar to coat well, pressing lightly. Cut ½″ off tips of four Kisses for eyes and ears; cut ¼″ off tips of remaining Kiss for nose. Press two eyes into frosting with flat side up. Press edge of each ear into frosting near top of cookies, flat side forward. Press edge of nose into frosting below eyes, pointed end downward. Use chocolate sprinkles for mouth. Attach a candy eyeball to each eye with frosting.

*Buy cookies or make homemade ones using Sugar Cookies recipe on page 62.

continued on next page

Puppy

Frost cookie and press two candy eyeballs in place. Use a brown peanut M&M for the nose and bend two short strips of red Rips into a mouth shape. Cut a pink jelly bean as desired for the tongue and press in place. Set Tootsie Rolls on waxed paper and microwave for 7 to 10 seconds until slightly softened. Shape candies into two ears and add to puppy's face.

Chick

Frost cookie and sprinkle with yellow sugar. Press five candy wafers into frosting at top of cookie, fanning them. Add two candy eyeballs. Cut another yellow candy wafer in half for wings and press in place, cut edge down. Cut one Chewy Cube into a beak shape and set in frosting, pointed end down. Cut a second Chewy Cube in thirds and use two of them for feet, slicing "claws" with kitchen shears; press into frosting.

Brownie Boom-Boom Tree

Spread chocolate frosting over thick fudgy brownies* or standard cupcakes. Sprinkle with graham cracker crumbs. Set leaf-shaped spearmint gumdrops on sugar-covered waxed paper. Flatten each leaf with a rolling pin until 2½″ long. For each tree, poke one end of a toothpick through three or four leaves near largest end; do not poke completely through top leaf. Rotate leaves until evenly spaced around top of toothpick.

Just before serving, press a chocolate hazelnut Pirouette Rolled Wafer into each brownie. Slide toothpick with leaves down into center of each Pirouette. Stack malted milk ball "coconuts" under each palm tree.

*Example uses 1 (18.3 oz.) package fudge brownie mix, baked in an 8 x 8″ pan.

Cheesy Monsters

You'll Need

- 2 (8 oz.) pkgs. cream cheese, softened, divided
- 3 C. finely shredded Cheddar cheese, divided
- 1 (1 oz.) pkg. ranch dressing mix
- Sliced provolone cheese
- Black and/or green olives
- Red bell pepper
- Thin pretzel sticks
- Other items as desired, such as pickles and/or pickled baby corn

Make It

1. Reserve a spoonful of cream cheese and 1¼ cups Cheddar cheese for later use. In a medium bowl, mix remaining cream cheese, 1¾ cups Cheddar cheese and dressing mix. Shape by heaping tablespoonful into 1½″ balls. Roll in reserved Cheddar cheese and set on a waxed paper-lined cookie sheet. Chill for 30 minutes.

2. Using a screw-on cap from flavoring extract or soda, cut small circles of provolone cheese for eyeballs. Slice olives and bell pepper to make mouths, eye pupils and other features. To assemble, break pretzels to desired length and poke into cheese balls; attach eye circles with some reserved cream cheese. Add other features to make each one monstrously silly. Serve promptly. Makes about 18 little monsters.

   Tip: *Use a drinking straw to cut out small circles of bell pepper or black olive for noses or pupils on monster eyes.*

Flower Power

You'll Need

1 (16.5 oz.) tube refrigerated sugar cookie dough*

Powdered sugar

8˝ plastic ice cream bucket lid

3½˝ round cookie cutter

Royal Icing**

Paste food coloring as desired**

2 T. chocolate frosting

Pastry bags fitted with small or medium round tips

Make It

1. Preheat oven to 350°. Let cookie dough soften at room temperature for 15 minutes. Shape half of dough into a round disk; dust with powdered sugar. Roll dough into a 10˝ circle, using more powdered sugar to prevent sticking. Cut a large circle with the plastic lid; re-roll dough scraps and cut a 3½˝ circle. With a pizza cutter, slice large circle into eight even wedges. Transfer wedges and circle to parchment paper-lined cookie sheet, leaving space between cookies. Bake for 10 to 12 minutes or until just starting to brown. Remove from oven and gently press spatula against wedge edges to straighten. Cool completely. Repeat steps to make a second flower cookie.

2. For each flower, tint about ¾ cup Royal Icing and frost "petals." While wet, spoon some white icing onto each petal point and drag a toothpick through icing toward wide end. Spread chocolate frosting on both round cookies. Let all cookies dry.

3. To assemble each flower, arrange petals in a flower shape with curved outer edges even (points will not touch in the middle). Set chocolate cookie over center and pipe white icing dots. Makes 2 large flowers.

   Or use Sugar Cookies recipe on page 62.

   **Example uses pink food coloring with Royal Icing recipe on page 62.

Phil & His Shadow

To make the groundhog's head, fasten the flat sides of two Dove candies together with chocolate frosting, edges even. Use frosting to attach two pearl dragees or round white sprinkles to head for eyeballs. Cut off ends of three chocolate-covered raisins for a nose and ears; attach to head with frosting. Attach two white sprinkle "teeth" below nose. With a toothpick, draw a "pupil" dot on each eyeball using frosting or black food coloring; let dry 15 minutes. Spread chocolate frosting around the hole in a fudge marshmallow cookie and set groundhog into it. Attach two chocolate-covered raisins underneath head to look like front paws; let dry.

Mice in the Puddin'

Remove leaves from clean dry strawberries. Coat berries in melted white almond bark and set on waxed paper to dry. Trim off excess hardened bark as needed. Working with one berry at a time, coat again in melted bark; press a round pink sprinkle "nose" into wet bark near pointed end of berry and add two chocolate sprinkle "eyes." Set almond slice "ears" on edge into bark about halfway back on strawberry; hold until set. Spoon chocolate pudding into dessert cups and set a mouse in each cup. Add a Rips Whips "tail" and a wedge of yellow fruit snack ("cheese") to each cup. Serve promptly.

Sweet Snails

You'll Need

Toothpicks
Mini marshmallows
Writing icing, any color

1 (13 oz.) tube *flaky cinnamon or caramel rolls (with icing)**

Make It

1. Preheat oven to 375°. To make eyes, poke a toothpick into the rounded side of each marshmallow and use a dot of writing icing to draw "pupils" on one flat side. Make a matching pair of eyes for each snail; let dry.

2. Separate rolls and place on a parchment paper-lined cookie sheet, 3˝ apart; set icing aside. Uncoil a 3˝ strip from the end of each roll and pull it away slightly for snail's head. Bake for 10 to 12 minutes or until golden brown. Cool for 10 minutes. Spoon icing over center of snail and insert two toothpick eyes in each head. Makes 8 snails.

Snails must be made with spiraled dough.

Change it Up

Whimsical Snakes: Uncoil each cinnamon roll and wind dough strip in a spiral around a clean 3/8˝ x 12˝ wood dowel. Bake on parchment paper-lined cookie sheet about 10 minutes. Cool slightly and slide dowel out of "snake." Drizzle with icing and add toothpick eyes.

Acorns & Leaves

Acorns: Used melted chocolate almond bark to attach one unwrapped chocolate Kiss to the flat side of each mini vanilla wafer. When set, use melted peanut butter candy wafers to attach a butterscotch chip to the other side. Let dry.

Leaves: Melt yellow, red, orange and/or tan candy wafers, stirring until smooth. Set mini twist pretzels on waxed paper and cover with melted candy. Set small pieces of pretzel sticks or twists into wet candy at heart-shaped end for stems. Drag a toothpick through candy to make "veins" in each leaf. Let dry.

Sing Out Loud

In a large saucepan over medium heat, stir together ¼ cup butter and 40 regular marshmallows until melted. Stir in 5 cups crisp rice cereal. With buttered hands, shape ½-cup portions of cereal mixture into eight balls, pressing well. Let cool and reshape as needed. Pour some M&Ms into eight standard ice cream cones. Spread white frosting around top edge of one cone and top with a cereal ball. Frost ball generously and coat with silver decorating sprinkles. Set in a mini muffin pan to dry. Repeat with remaining cones and cereal balls. Before serving, poke a small hole in the bottom of each cone and insert a Good & Plenty (or Mike and Ike) candy for cordless antenna. Makes 8 microphones.

Lunchtime Pals

You'll Need

Assorted cookie cutters

Sliced white sandwich bread

Sliced wheat sandwich bread

Sliced pumpernickel cocktail bread

Sandwich filling (peanut butter, flavored cream cheese, sliced cheese, jam, etc.)

Soft butter and/or peanut butter

Black olives

Sliced provolone cheese (bull and dog only)

Red bell pepper (dog only)

Make It

For all animals: Use cookie cutters, drinking straws and a serrated knife to cut bread as directed. Spread sandwich filling on one "head" piece and set matching piece on top with edges even before attaching details with butter or peanut butter.

Cow & Bull

Cut off ¾″ from opposite sides of two slices of white bread; trim crust off top and bottom to make two rectangles. Trim off corners to complete head shape and sandwich together with filling. From pumpernickel bread, cut two 1½″ football shapes for ears and one 2″ muzzle using a number 8-shaped cookie cutter (or use similar shape and cut nostril holes with a straw). With a straw, cut two eyes from pumpernickel bread. Cut a 3″ oval from cheese and attach at mouth end of head, extending over edges. Attach ears, eyes and muzzle. To make a bull, insert narrow pointed horns (about 2″ long, cut from pumpernickel crusts) and trim an olive slice into a "C" shape to place in nostril holes.

Pig

Cut two 4″ circles from white bread and sandwich together with filling. From pumpernickel bread, cut two 1½″ ears with a bell cookie cutter (or similar shape) and cut a 1½″ round snout. With a straw, cut two holes from snout. Use the straw to cut two eyes from an olive. Gently press eyes into bread and attach nose and ears.

continued on next page

Bear

Cut two 3½" to 4" circles from wheat bread and sandwich together with filling. From wheat bread, cut two 1½" round ears. From white bread, cut one 1¾" to 2" round muzzle and cut two small eyes with a drinking straw or knife. From pumpernickel bread, cut two 1" circles; slice off the bottom third for dark eye circles. Attach muzzle to head. Attach eye circles above muzzle, straight edge down. Fasten small white eyes to eye circles. For nose, cut one olive in half lengthwise and press into muzzle. Cut two olives slices into "C" shapes and set on muzzle for mouth. At top of head, insert ear circles partway into filling.

Dog

Trim off top and bottom crusts from two slices of wheat bread. Trim off sides at a slight angle and round off lower corners for dog's head; sandwich together with filling. Cut one 1¾" diamond from wheat bread and then cut in half for two triangle ears. From white bread, cut two 1" round "cheeks." From provolone cheese, cut two 1" eye circles. Cut a tapered tongue from red pepper, about ¾" long. From an olive, cut a nose and two small eye slivers. Set nose and tongue on head and attach cheeks on each side, overlapping those pieces. Attach eye circles and set olive slivers on top to finish eyes. Attach ears to side of "head."

Donut Snowmen Party

Press one candy corn into the hole of each mini powdered sugar donut for a carrot nose. Use white writing gel to attach mini dark chocolate chips for eyes and mouth. Make each snowman's expression different!

To make **Rudolph Donuts,** press a cherry sour ball or red peanut M&M into the hole of each mini chocolate donut for a red nose. Break pretzels (stick or mini twists) to create antlers and poke ends into the top of donut. Attach candy eyeballs with chocolate frosting.

Palm Tree Paradise

You'll Need

2 kiwifruit, peeled (or 1 green apple)

2 clementines, peeled

1 banana, peeled

½ yellow apple, optional

Make it

1. Cut each kiwifruit into at least eight lengthwise wedges. Separate clementines into segments. Trim off both ends of banana and slice it in half lengthwise. Brush with lemon juice and blot dry with paper towels.

2. Arrange banana halves on a plate, cut side down, to resemble two palm tree trunks bending in the breeze. Arrange kiwi wedges on top of each trunk to look like palms. Set clementine sections below the tree trunks.

3. To make the sun, cut yellow apple into a half circle. Cut thin pointed wedges for sun's rays. Brush with lemon juice and blot dry. Arrange apple pieces above clementines, skin side up, to look like a setting sun.

Change it Up

Tattooed Bananas: Use a toothpick to mark the skin of a yellow banana with a secret message. Try not to poke through the skin. Within a short time, the message will magically turn brown.

Clementine Punkin: Peel a clementine and insert a piece of celery or green Mike and Ike Fruit Twist into the center for a stem.

Garden Pops

You'll Need

4˝ white lollipop sticks
Regular marshmallows
Blue candy melts
Finely crushed chocolate cookie crumbs
Flower-shaped decorating sprinkles
Green decorating sprinkles, optional

Make It

Push a stick into the top of a marshmallow, past the center but not through top. Melt ½ cup candy melts according to package directions and let cool slightly. Dip marshmallow into melted candy, covering base of stick. Tap stick lightly to let excess candy drip off. Immediately press end and edges of marshmallow into ½ cup cookie crumbs and press flower sprinkles into wet bark. Add green sprinkle "stems" if desired. Set on waxed paper to dry. Repeat to make about 8 pops.

Change it Up

Swim Little Fishy: Coat marshmallows in melted blue candy as directed, but dip ends in graham cracker crumbs. Press a goldfish cracker or gummy fish into wet bark. Add two round white sprinkles for bubbles.

Holiday Mallows: Coat marshmallows in any color melted candy. Dip ends in sprinkling sugar or colored decorating sprinkles to match the holiday theme. Press gourmet holiday candies, sprinkles or cake decorations into wet bark.

Nesting Pretzel Chicks

Melt ½ cup yellow candy melts according to package directions. Set mini twist pretzels on waxed paper and fill center of each with melted candy; swirl top to look like feathers or wings. With two rounded sides of pretzels at the top, set a small chocolate sprinkle "eye" into wet candy. Use orange icing and a small round tip to pipe a beak over pretzel nob near eye. Let dry. Makes about 20.

To make a nest, melt a few peanut butter candy melts to attach pretzels. Fasten three pretzel sticks together to make a triangle base. Randomly stack and attach pretzels (whole ones and halves) to build a nest, leaving center area open. Let dry. Set chicks in nest.

Tweets in a Tree

Place one clean celery rib (with leaves) on a serving plate. Cook small frozen meatballs according to package directions. Poke a little hole in the center of each meatball and insert a carrot sliver "beak." Attach two whole allspice "eyes" with a bit of squeeze cheese. Swirl cooked spaghetti over the center of celery to look like a nest; fill with hot spaghetti sauce and set meatball "birds" in nest.

Grillin' Fun

You'll Need

Round red apples*
Pretzel rods
Creamy peanut butter
Small Butterfinger candy bar, crushed
Chocolate or black icing
Pastry bag fitted with small round piping tip
Candies (fruit-shaped gummy snacks or other chewy candies and Caramel Creams)
Black edible marker

Make It

1. Slice off the bottom third of an apple and discard or eat it. Brush cut side of remaining apple piece with lemon juice and blot dry with paper towels. Break off three 2½″ "legs" from ends of pretzel rods; discard center pieces. Carefully push a toothpick halfway into broken end of each pretzel piece. To attach tripod legs to the "grill," slide toothpicks with pretzels into apple around stem end, evenly spaced and angled out so apple sets level.

2. Spread peanut butter on cut side of apple; sprinkle with Butterfinger crumbs. Pipe lines of icing over peanut butter to look like a grate. Push candies onto toothpick "skewers" and draw "grill lines" on candy with edible marker. Mold Caramel Creams to look like meat and draw lines on top. Set skewers and meat on the grate. Eat promptly.

Example uses Jazz apples.

Change it Up

Apple Racers: Dip red, green or yellow apple wedges into lemon juice for the race car bodies; blot dry. Slice grapes in half. With toothpicks, attach grape "wheels" to front and back of car, cut side out. Cut off any excess toothpick.

Green Goblin Grins

With small cookie cutters or a sharp knife, cut red bell peppers into fun tongue shapes, ½″ to 1″ in size. Cut a slit through the top side only of sugar snap peas or pea pods, starting and ending about ½″ from ends. If peas inside pod are large, carefully remove several to make room for the tongue. Slide a tongue into the slit, smooth side down. Insert slivered almond "teeth" in slit and share a grin!

Grampa's Chompers

Cut a large red apple in half through the core. Slice each half into crosswise wedges. Trim out the core from each wedge with a small round cookie cutter. Brush all cut edges with lemon juice and blot dry with paper towels. Pair up matching apple "lips" and spread peanut butter on inside cut edges. Line up mini marshmallow "teeth" along lower lip and set matching lip on top, peanut butter side down; press together lightly. Makes 5 or 6 sets.

For extra giggles: Leave a few teeth out or use black or yellow edible markers to draw braces or cavities on teeth.

Fruity Blooms

You'll Need

- 1 (3 oz.) pkg. cream cheese, softened
- 1 (6 oz.) container strawberry Greek yogurt
- 3 T. sugar or brown sugar
- 5 small plastic condiment cups
- 1 fresh pineapple
- 4˝ flower-shaped metal cookie cutter
- 1˝ round metal cookie cutter, optional
- 3 kiwifruit
- Chocolate decorating sprinkles

Make It

1. In a small bowl, beat together cream cheese, yogurt and sugar until smooth. Divide among condiment cups and chill until needed.

2. Cut off bottom and top of pineapple; slice crosswise into 1˝-thick disks. Press flower-shaped cookie cutter down on each disk to cut flowers; discard pineapple skins. With round cookie cutter or sharp knife, cut out center core of each flower; discard. Set flowers on paper towels to drain. Peel each kiwifruit and slice crosswise into five or six rounds, about ⅜˝ thick. Cut rounds in half for flower petals. Set pineapple flowers on serving plates and insert dip cups. Arrange overlapping kiwifruit petals around dip cup and garnish with pineapple leaves. Just before serving, top dip with sprinkles. Makes 5 flowers.

Berry Jolly Cupcake Topper

You'll Need

Large pointed strawberries   Mini cupcakes*

and..

For Christmas Trees: 1 tube green decorating icing fitted with star decorating tip, decorating sprinkles (yellow flowers or stars, multi-colored round)

For Santa's Hats: white frosting, pastry bag fitted with medium flower or closed star tip, mini marshmallows

Make It

For Both Projects: Remove strawberry leaves but don't cut fruit.

Tree

Attach stem end of strawberry to top of cupcake with some icing. Press icing tip against lower edge of berry near cupcake and squeeze tube while pulling out and down to lay a bough-like ribbon of icing on berry and cupcake. Make a row of "pine tree boughs" around strawberry. Make another row just above first one and repeat until berry is covered. Set a yellow sprinkle on top of "tree" and decorate boughs with colored sprinkles. Let dry.

Hat

Place frosting in pastry bag and pipe several rings of frosting around top of cupcake until about ¾˝ deep (leave center unfrosted). Set stem end of strawberry in center of frosting ring. Add one more ring of frosting around berry and attach a marshmallow to tip of "hat" with frosting. Chill until serving time.

Examples use white cupcakes in red and brown liners.

Treasure Chest Cookies

You'll Need

1 batch Sugar Cookies dough (recipe on page 62)

Large and small cookie cutters*

1 (7 oz.) pouch cookie icing

Small candies (such as mini M&Ms or Nerds)

Frosting, royal icing** and/or decorating sprinkles as desired

Make It

1. Preheat oven to 400°. Divide dough in half and shape portions into flat disks; refrigerate one disk until needed. On lightly floured parchment paper, roll out remaining disk to ⅛″ to ¼″ thickness. With large cookie cutter, cut two matching shapes for each "treasure chest," rerolling dough as needed. Transfer to parchment paper-lined cookie sheets and bake for 7 to 8 minutes. Cool on pan for 2 minutes; transfer to wire rack to cool completely.

2. Let chilled dough warm up slightly and roll out to ⅜″ thickness. With large cookie cutter, cut one thick cookie to match each treasure chest, rerolling dough as needed. Use small cutter to cut out the middle of each thick cookie, leaving a ½″ rim. Transfer to cookie sheets and bake for 10 to 12 minutes. Let cool.

3. To assemble, group two thin cookies with a matching thick one. With icing, attach the bottom of thick cookie to top of one thin cookie, edges even. Fill middle with candies. Attach remaining thin cookie on top with icing. Decorate cookies with frosting, royal icing and/or sprinkles as desired.

Use 2½″ to 4″ cookie cutters (egg, gift and heart shapes), plus 1½″ cutters (round, oval or matching shapes) to cut openings in thick cookies.

** Try Royal Icing recipe on page 62.

Tip: *If opening in cookie shrinks during baking, recut centers while cookies are still warm.*

Mugging with Frosty

With kitchen shears, cut regular (or jumbo) marshmallows in half crosswise, trying to maintain a round shape. Dip cut sides in powdered sugar and shake off excess; set cut side down on waxed paper. Use black writing icing to make dots for the eyes and mouth. With orange icing and a round piping tip, draw a carrot nose that's thicker in the center and narrows into a point toward one side. Let dry slightly before floating in mugs of hot chocolate.

Hedgehog Babies

Unwrap and cut a chewy caramel into three pieces; flatten each piece to make a face shape. Frost three small mint patties with chocolate frosting and set a face on each one. Coat exposed frosting with chocolate decorating sprinkles, pressing lightly in place. Press small sprinkle pieces into caramel face for nose and eyes. Makes 3 hedgehogs.

What a Hoot!

You'll Need

1 roll Peanut Butter-Chocolate Cookies dough (recipe on page 63)

Whole cashews

White writing icing or chocolate frosting

Hershey's Milk Chocolate Drops

Make It

1. Let chilled dough soften at room temperature for 20 minutes. Preheat oven to 350°. Cut dough into ¼″ to ⅜″-thick slices. Reshape with hands until evenly round. Set two slices side by side on parchment paper-lined cookie sheets; press them together in the center. Pinch top corners to make pointed "ears." Press a cashew into the center for each beak. Bake for 8 to 10 minutes. Remove from oven; if beaks have drooped during baking, reposition cashews. Cool on pan for 2 minutes; transfer to wire rack to cool completely.

2. With icing, attach Chocolate Drop "eyes" to peanut butter centers of each cookie. (For a sleepy owl, cut candy in half and attach pieces horizontally near the bottom, cut side up. For a surprised owl, place halves vertically in the center, cut side against cookie.) Makes about 16 owls.

Change it up

Make **Dog Face Cookies** from a roll of Peanut Butter-Chocolate dough. Tear off pieces of dough and shape into ears. Press ears onto a dough slice and bake as directed. When cool, add "Husky" eyes with icing and blue sprinkles or attach mini brown M&Ms with chocolate frosting. Use frosting or a brown M&M or Almond Joy piece for the nose and pipe on a mouth.

Ahoy Maties!

You'll Need

1 C. vanilla frosting

Chocolate frosting, divided

6 cupcakes, any flavor

1 (3.3 oz.) pkg. AirHeads (6 bars)

Candy eyeballs

Black Jujyfruit candies

Pink or red Mini Chewy SweeTARTS

Chocolate decorating sprinkles

Pastry bag fitted with leaf or star tip

Black decorating icing

Mini M&Ms, optional

Make It

1. Stir together vanilla frosting with enough chocolate frosting to create desired face color; frost cupcakes. With kitchen shears, cut a bandana or hat shape from AirHeads for each pirate; set into frosting on pirate's "head." Cut small mouths from red AirHead scraps.

2. Place one candy eyeball on each pirate face and one Jujyfruit "patch" where other eyeball should be. Set a SweeTART "nose" and AirHead "mouth" in place. For beards and mustaches, scatter chocolate sprinkles on face and/or use pastry bag to pipe on chocolate frosting. Pipe a line of black icing at an angle for the patch cord. If desired, attach M&M spots to bandana with vanilla frosting. Serve the same day. Makes 6 pirates.

Change it Up

To make **Pete the Parrot**, bake a cupcake in a green paper liner and frost with green icing. Cut an AirHead hat or bandana and set on parrot's "head." Use a whole cashew for a beak. Draw two large eye spots with white icing. Place a mini brown M&M on one eye spot and a black Jujyfruit on other spot; let icing set up. Pipe on a black icing patch cord.

Mellow Mallow Teddy Bears

You'll Need

- Regular marshmallows
- 4˝ or 8˝ white lollipop sticks
- White almond bark
- Mini marshmallows
- Finely crushed graham cracker crumbs
- Sugar
- Mini brown M&Ms
- Mini chocolate chips
- Black writing gel

Make It

1. For each bear, slide two regular marshmallows onto a stick, flat sides lined up and facing forward; do not pierce top of marshmallow "head." Melt bark according to package directions. Dip an edge of four mini marshmallows into melted bark and attach to bear's body for paws. Attach two more mini marshmallows to top of head for ears. Cut one mini marshmallow in half and attach one half to "face" for a muzzle. Let dry.

2. In a small bowl, mix ½ cup cracker crumbs and 1 tablespoon sugar. One at a time, dip bears into cold water and promptly coat with crumb mixture. Shake off excess and let dry on waxed paper.

3. Remelt bark to attach one M&M to each muzzle and one chocolate chip "belly button" to each body. Poke a toothpick hole for each eye and add a drop of writing gel; let dry.

Change it Up

To make **Gingerbread Man**, follow directions above to attach marshmallow limbs, but omit ears and muzzle. Dip in water and coat figures in a mixture of ½ cup sugar, 2 teaspoons ground cinnamon and ½ teaspoon ground ginger. When dry, use black and white writing gels to draw eyes and mouth. Attach candy sprinkle buttons to body with melted bark.

A "Pear" of Eagles

You'll Need

- 2 red Anjou or Bosc pears
- 2 cubes white almond bark
- 10 whole cashews, divided
- 4 mini dark chocolate chips
- ½ C. toasted coconut*
- 2 tsp. sweetened flaked coconut (white, not toasted)
- 6 Caramel Creams, unwrapped
- ½ cube chocolate almond bark

Make It

1. Rinse and dry pears well; remove stems. Set on a flat surface to find front of each "eagle." With a sharp knife, cut a hole about 1¼˝ from the top, just large enough to hold a cashew. Blot juice inside holes with a paper towel; set aside.

2. Melt white bark according to package directions; let cool slightly. Working with one pear at a time, coat top ⅔ of fruit in melted bark, letting excess drip off. While bark is still wet, insert a cashew in hole and set two chocolate chip "eyes" in place. Quickly press toasted coconut "feathers" into lower part of wet bark. Sprinkle top of head with white coconut. Let dry.

3. On waxed paper, press three Caramel Creams together for each triangle-shaped "perch" (with two caramels in front). Make a shallow dent in each perch where eagle will rest. Melt chocolate bark and spoon some on top of perch; place eagle in wet bark and hold until set. Press two pairs of cashew "talons" into wet bark at front of each perch. Let dry. Makes 2 eagles.

   *To toast, spread coconut in a shallow pan and bake at 375° for 6 to 8 minutes or until well browned, stirring once. Let cool.

King of the Jungle

In a zippered plastic bag, combine 1 cup sweetened flaked coconut with 1 tablespoon unsweetened cocoa powder; shake until well coated. Mix 1⅓ cups vanilla frosting with yellow food coloring and frost 12 (3″) sugar cookies.* Decorate each cookie with mini brown M&M "eyes" and a Junior Caramel or Mint "nose." Press coated coconut into frosting around edge of cookies. Set two Hershey's Milk Chocolate Drops in place for ears. Cut slivers of black twist licorice for whiskers and set in place. Pipe thin lines of black icing to make mouths. Makes 12 lions.

*Buy cookies or use Sugar Cookies recipe on page 62.

Potato Head Parade

Mix vanilla frosting with a bit of chocolate frosting; stir in tiny amounts of yellow and red paste food coloring until color resembles Mr. Potato Head. Spread frosting on standard cupcakes, any flavor. Use unwrapped candies and sprinkles to decorate each face differently, cutting candies as needed. Use mini M&Ms, candy eyeballs, fruit slices, spice drops, Jujyfruits, Maple Nut Goodies, cherry sours, Good & Plenty, Sprees, white York Pieces, Smarties (small and large), Chewy SweeTARTS, gumballs, chocolate and black twist licorice, decorating sprinkles and peppermint patties. Let dry and set cupcakes on edge to serve.

50

A-Nutter Giraffe

You'll Need

Melted chocolate or white almond bark (or peanut butter candy wafers)

Candy eyeballs

Nutter Butter cookies

Mini vanilla wafers

Mini M&Ms (brown, red, yellow, orange)

Mini twist pretzels

Pretzel sticks

Caramel Creams

Long pretzel rods

Make It

1. Use melted bark to attach all pieces, remelting as needed. Attach two candy eyeballs to each cookie, about ¾″ from top. Attach a vanilla wafer to lower end of cookie; then attach two brown M&M "nostrils." To make a mouth or tongue, break off a small curved piece of twist pretzel or cut red M&M in half; attach to wafer and let dry.

2. Break pretzel sticks into 1″ pieces for "horns." Cut a Caramel Cream into wedges; flatten and form each wedge into an ear shape with cream filling intact. Set horns and ears aside. Attach a pretzel rod "neck" to back side of cookie with plenty of bark, placing top of pretzel at least ½″ below top of cookie; hold until set. Using more bark on the back of cookie, attach two horns above pretzel rod and attach an ear at each side of "head"; hold until set. With giraffe face up, attach a yellow or orange M&M to top of each horn, holding until set.

Bottoms-Up Bunnies

With melted white almond bark, attach two white York Pieces to each Raffaello Almond Coconut Treat for back paws; hold until set. Use pink icing* to make small "pads" on each paw; set "bunnies" in mini muffin pan to dry. Spoon about 2 tablespoons chocolate cookie crumbs into clear 5-ounce cups. Add chocolate pudding and sprinkle more crumbs on top for "dirt." Push orange Mike and Ike candies halfway into dirt like a row of carrots. With green decorating icing, pipe a carrot "top" on each one; let dry. Set a bunny in each cup, feet end up. Spoon stiff white frosting into a pastry bag fitted with a star tip and pipe a fluffy tail on each bunny.

*Example uses a 7-ounce pouch of pink cookie icing.

Daschund Darling

Use melted white almond bark to attach a pastel candy corn "ear" to both flat sides of one regular marshmallow "head"; let dry. Push a piece of uncooked spaghetti through the middle of five regular marshmallows for dog's body. Cut a regular marshmallow in half lengthwise and then cut into several pointed wedges. Attach one larger wedge to the front of dog's head using spaghetti reinforced with melted bark; hold until set. In the same way, attach a small wedge "tail" and four mini marshmallow "feet" to the body. With spaghetti and bark, attach head to body; attach a mini brown M&M "nose" and two candy eyeballs with bark.

Monster Cups

You'll Need

Permanent or paint markers

4 (5 oz.) clear plastic glasses

1 (3 to 3.4 oz.) pkg. vanilla pudding mix* (instant or cook & serve)

2 C. milk

Liquid food coloring, optional

Sweetened flaked coconut, decorating sprinkles or cookie crumbs

Make It

1 With markers, draw a face on the outside of each glass; let dry.

2 Combine pudding mix with milk according to package instructions. If desired, stir in food coloring. Divide mixture among glasses, about ½ cup each.

3 Sprinkle tops with coconut, sprinkles or crumbs. Serve with a spoon. Makes 4 monsters.

*Try other pudding flavors such as coconut cream, banana cream, white chocolate or cheesecake.

Change it Up

To make **Cereal Cup Monsters**, cut a regular marshmallow in half crosswise for two eyeballs. Press the pointed side of a dark chocolate chip (any size) into the sticky cut side of each eyeball and press against the inside of a 10-ounce clear plastic glass. Fill with cereal such as Kix, Cheerios or Fruit Loops.

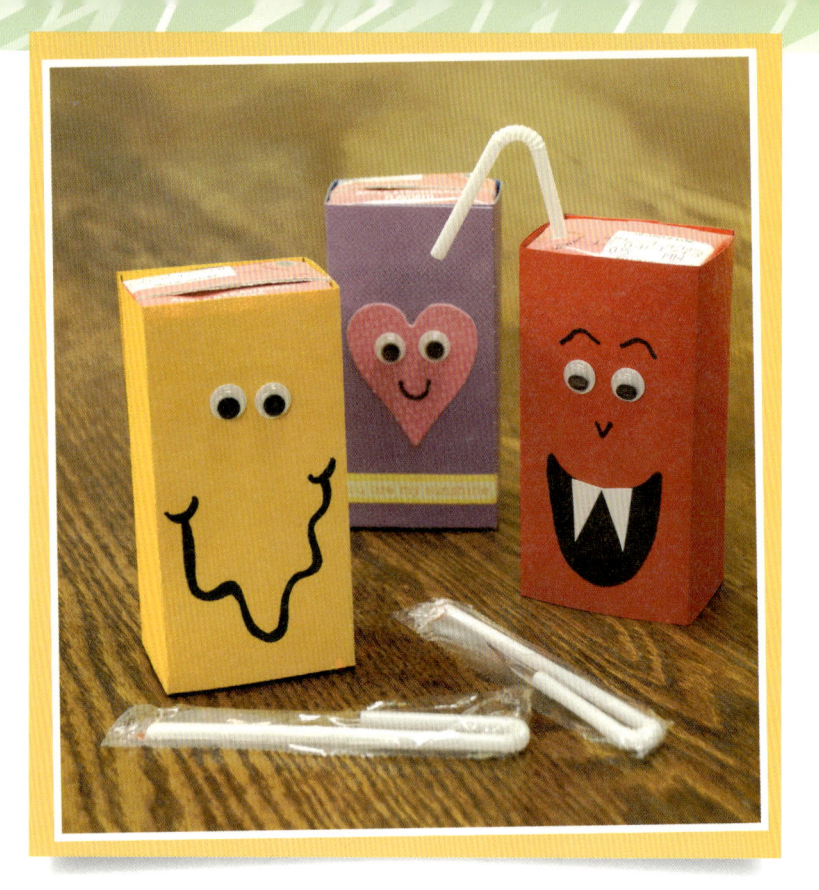

Juice Box Jokesters

Cut a rectangle of construction or scrapbooking paper about 8˝ wide and the height of a juice box. Wrap the paper around the box, overlapping it on the back side and creasing corners well; fasten with double-stick tape or glue. With markers, draw a face on the front side of box and attach wobbly plastic eyeballs with glue. Add stickers, if desired.

Tip: *For clean creases, measure the juice box sides and draw heavy pencil lines on the back side of paper where each corner will be; fold along these score lines.*

Tiny and Tasty

Itty Bitty Feast

Cut a chocolate hazelnut Pirouette Rolled Wafer into four 1½" pieces. Attach "table legs" to one side of a chocolate graham cracker rectangle with melted chocolate almond bark; let dry. Brush flat side of mini vanilla wafers with light corn syrup for the plates. On each wet plate, place two sliced almonds ("turkey"), a few green and orange Celebration Deco sprinkles ("peas and carrots") and a blob of white frosting ("mashed potatoes"). Add yellow decorating sprinkles or a drop of caramel topping to potatoes for butter or gravy. Set plates on the "table" and add a centerpiece, like a candy pumpkin surrounded by toasted coconut and fall-colored mini M&Ms or a Fruit Roll-Up "cloth" and a Bugle chip "cornucopia" filled with mini M&Ms.

continued on next page

Eggs & Bacon: Melt white almond bark and drop by spoonful onto waxed paper. Set a yellow M&M or chewy Spree candy "yolk" in wet bark. Break a pretzel stick in half and press in wet bark for bacon; let dry.

Hot Diggity Dogs: Cut a Circus Peanut lengthwise (but not through) for the hot dog bun. Roll a Milk Maid Royal caramel into a hot dog shape, covering the filling at each end. Set in "bun" and top with red and/or yellow writing icing for ketchup and mustard. Add tiny pieces of green and/or yellow Rips Whips for pickle relish and onions. (For foot-long hot dogs, use chewy caramels.)

Pixie Donuts & Cup O' Joe: Coat Cheerios cereal with melted chocolate or white almond bark and top with tiny sprinkles or colored sugar; let dry. Toss more cereal with powdered sugar. For each coffee cup, push a mini brown M&M into the wide end of a spice drop. Cut a center slice from a second spice drop, cut in half and cut into a "C" shape. Attach sticky ends of "handle" to side of cup.

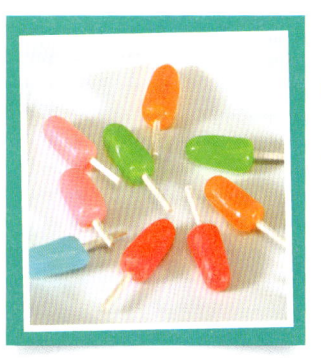

Petite Popsicles: Poke a toothpick into the wide end of a Mike and Ike candy; trim toothpick to about ½˝. To make ice cream bars, dip each one in melted dark chocolate candy wafers and let dry.

Baby Ice Cream Cones: Scoop cold buttercream frosting with a small melon baller and mold lightly with fingers to look like scoops of ice cream. Set into Bugles chips. Add food coloring, crushed cookies or decorating sprinkles to the frosting for different "flavors."

Stop & Go: Cut celery into 3˝ lengths. Using the large end of a metal frosting tip, cut circles of red, yellow and green bell pepper for the "lights"; drain on paper towels. Fill celery with soft cream cheese (plain or flavored). Line up a red, yellow and green circle in cream cheese.

Quick and Cute

Dandy Dominoes: Cut graham crackers into small rectangles along score lines. Spread white frosting smoothly on each rectangle. Drag a toothpick across center to mark halfway line. Press matching mini M&Ms on each half to look like dominoes. Let dry.

Something to Crow About: Cut black twist licorice into 1˝ slivers for feathers. Attach two candy eyeballs to a chocolate sandwich cookie with chocolate frosting. Press licorice pieces into the filling between cookies so feathers stick up from "head." With orange decorating icing and a round or leaf tip, draw a beak; let dry.

Apple a Day: Coat both sides of a mini twist pretzel in melted red candy wafers, letting excess drip off. Set on waxed paper. Press a small piece of green Rips Whips into wet coating at the top for a stem. If desired, cut a "leaf" from green Rips and add on top.

Sailing Over the Ocean Blue: Peel a tangerine and separate into two-segment pieces to make "boats." Cut triangular "sails" from a Fruit Roll-Up; press one short edge around a 5˝ plastic coffee stirrer straw. Trim end of straws to 2˝ and slide between segments through bottom of boats. Set boats on Berry Blue Jello snack cups, pressing straw lightly into gelatin.

Be-Jeweled: Attach a Fruit Gusher "jewel" to a Snackwell Yogurt Pretzel with a bit of melted white almond bark. Hold until set, then let dry completely.

61

Recipes

Royal Icing

3 T. meringue powder
4 C. sifted powdered sugar

Paste food coloring as instructed in project

In a medium mixing bowl, beat together meringue powder, powdered sugar and 6 tablespoons warm water on medium-high speed for 7 to 10 minutes or until icing is smooth and soft peaks form. Stir in food coloring. To thicken (for piping), stir in a little more powdered sugar. To thin (for flooding and frosting large areas), stir in a few drops of warm water.

Used for Flower Power on page 10 and Treasure Chest Cookies on page 36.

Sugar Cookies

1 C. butter, softened
1½ C. powdered sugar
1 egg
2 tsp. clear vanilla or almond extract
2½ C. flour, plus extra for adding and rolling
2 tsp. baking powder
1 tsp. salt

In a large mixing bowl, beat butter until creamy. Beat in powdered sugar. Add egg and vanilla; beat until well blended. In a separate bowl, whisk together 2½ cups flour, baking powder and salt. Add flour mixture to butter mixture and beat until dough forms. If sticky, stir in 1 to 2 tablespoons additional flour. Divide dough in half and shape into round disks; let rest several minutes or chill until needed. Roll out dough on lightly floured parchment paper. Cut dough into shapes and bake according to project directions.

Used for Treasure Chest Cookies on page 36 and King of the Jungle cookies on page 48.

Peanut Butter-Chocolate Cookies

6 T. butter, softened

6 T. creamy peanut butter

½ C. sugar

½ C. brown sugar

1 egg

1 tsp. vanilla extract

2½ C. flour

2 tsp. baking powder

½ tsp. salt

¼ C. unsweetened cocoa powder, plus more for rolling

In a large mixing bowl, beat butter until creamy. Beat in peanut butter, sugar and brown sugar until light and well blended. Add egg and vanilla; beat well. In a separate bowl, whisk together flour, baking powder and salt. Gradually add flour mixture to butter mixture and beat until well mixed. Shape dough into a fat log; cut off ⅔ of log and place in a bowl. Add ¼ cup cocoa powder to bowl and mix with a spoon until well blended. Dust a flat work surface with additional cocoa powder and roll out chocolate dough to make a rectangle about 4 x 10″. On a clean work surface, shape remaining peanut butter dough into a log about 10″ long. Set log in center of chocolate dough and wrap chocolate dough around peanut butter dough, sealing well. Roll on work surface until well rounded and smooth. Transfer to a 9 x 13″ baking pan, cover and refrigerate for 2 hours or overnight. Shape dough and bake according to project directions.

Used for What a Hoot! and Dog Face Cookies on pages 40-41.

Projects

A "Pear" of Eagles	46
Acorns & Leaves	16
Ahoy Maties!	42
A-Nutter Giraffe	50
Apple a Day	61
Apple Racers	29
Baby Ice Cream Cones	59
Be-Jeweled	61
Berry Jolly Cupcake Toppers	34
Bottoms-Up Bunnies	52
Brownie Boom-Boom Tree	7
Cereal Cup Monsters	55
Cheesy Monsters	8
Clementine Punkin	23
Cookie Critter Cuties	4
Dandy Dominoes	60
Daschund Darling	53
Dog Face Cookies	41
Donut Snowmen Party	21
Eggs & Bacon	58
Flower Power	10
Flutterbies	3
Fruity Blooms	32
Garden Pops	24
Gingerbread Man	45
Grampa's Chompers	31
Green Goblin Grins	30
Grillin' Fun	28
Hedgehog Babies	39
Holiday Mallows	25
Hot Diggity Dogs	58
Itty Bitty Feast	57
Juice Box Jokesters	56
King of the Jungle	48
Lunchtime Pals	18
Mellow Mallow Teddy Bears	44
Mice in the Puddin'	13
Monster Cups	54
Mugging with Frosty	38
Nesting Pretzel Chicks	26
Palm Tree Paradise	22
Pete the Parrot	43
Petite Popsicles	59
Phil & His Shadow	12
Pixie Donuts & Cup O' Joe	58
Potato Head Parade	49
Rudolph Donuts	21
Sailing Over the Ocean Blue	61
Sing Out Loud	17
Something to Crow About	60
Stop & Go	59
Sweet Snails	14
Swim Little Fishy	25
Tattooed Bananas	23
Treasure Chest Cookies	36
Tweets in a Tree	27
What a Hoot!	40
Whimsical Snakes	15

Recipes

Peanut Butter-Chocolate Cookies	63
Royal Icing	62
Sugar Cookies	62